Burrs to Velcro

Tech from Nature

By Jennifer Colby

21st Century
Junior Library

Published in the United States of America by
Cherry Lake Publishing
Ann Arbor, Michigan
www.cherrylakepublishing.com

Reading Adviser: Marla Conn, MS, Ed., Literacy specialist, Read-Ability, Inc.
Content Adviser: Rachel Brown, MA, Sustainable Business

Photo Credits: © Rachel Juliet Lerch/Shutterstock.com, Cover, 1 [left]; © raksapon/Shutterstock.com,
Cover, 1 [right]; © JW Company/Shutterstock.com, 4; © New Africa/Shutterstock.com, 6; © John Tann/Flickr, 8;
© Anton Watman/Shutterstock.com, 10; © KAE CH/Shutterstock.com, 12; © Stocksnapper/Shutterstock.com, 14;
© Fotos593/Shutterstock.com, 16; © Pixabay.com, 18; © icsnaps/Shutterstock.com, 20

Library of Congress Cataloging-in-Publication Data

Names: Colby, Jennifer, author.
Title: Burrs to Velcro / Jennifer Colby.
Description: Ann Arbor : Cherry Lake Publishing, 2019. | Includes bibliographical references and index. |
    Audience: Age 7-10. | Audience: Grade 4 to 6.
Identifiers: LCCN 2018035192 | ISBN 9781534142909 (hardcover) | ISBN 9781534140660 (pdf) |
    ISBN 9781534139466 (pbk.) | ISBN 9781534141865 (hosted ebook)
Subjects: LCSH: Fasteners—Juvenile literature. | Seeds—Dispersal—Juvenile literature.
Classification: LCC TT557 .C65 2019 | DDC 646/.19—dc23
LC record available at https://lccn.loc.gov/2018035192

Cherry Lake Publishing would like to acknowledge the work of the Partnership for 21st Century Skills.
Please visit *www.p21.org* for more information.

Printed in the United States of America
Corporate Graphics

CONTENTS

5 **Clever Connector**

7 **Fascinating Fasteners**

11 **Nuisance to Inspiration**

17 **All Kinds of Uses**

22 Glossary

23 Find Out More

24 Index

24 About the Author

Velcro has many different uses.

Clever Connector

When was the last time you used Velcro? You may have used it to close a flap on your backpack or your lunch bag. You may have used it in a game.

It is hard to imagine a time when Velcro didn't exist. What did people use before it was invented?

There are many different types of fasteners.

Fascinating Fasteners

People have used all kinds of **fasteners**. Buttons are common on shirts. But they are not very strong.

A belt is usually fastened with a **buckle**. They are strong, but heavy and expensive to make. Shoelaces are light and cheap. And they can tighten the entire shoe. But they take time to tie.

If you wear jeans or a jacket, then you

Nature has its own fastener.

have used a zipper. Zippers are fast and easy to use. But they get stuck sometimes.

What other fasteners do you use?

Have you ever gone on a hike? You might have noticed small, spiky objects sticking to your clothes. These are called burrs. Burrs can be difficult to remove. They can be a pain.

But burrs **inspired** a new invention. Velcro! How did something so **annoying** inspire something so useful? Let's find out.

Look!

Explore your neighborhood with an adult. See if you can find any burr plants. Take photos. Take notes. With the help of a librarian, research these plants further.

Burrs get stuck on things.

Nuisance to Inspiration

Burrs are annoying. But these pesky things are important to some plants. Plants cannot move on their own. They depend on something else to move their seeds around.

Some plants use burrs to spread their seeds. Burrs are fruits of the plant. They have seeds inside them. They are covered in tiny spikes that have hooks on the ends. Animals brush past the plants, and the

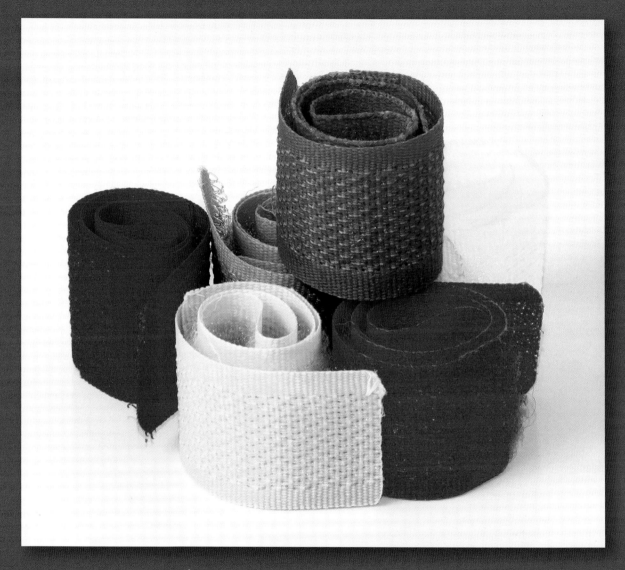

Velcro comes in many sizes and colors.

hooks get stuck in their fur. The burrs eventually fall off the animal. This spreads the plant's seeds!

In 1941, Frenchman George de Mestral took his dog for a walk. A large number of burrs stuck to his clothes as he hiked.

He looked at the **connection** of the burrs to his clothing. He noticed that the tiny hooks had caught on the threads of his clothes.

De Mestral had an idea! He would create two different pieces. One would have a hooked surface similar to the burr. The other

De Mestral created a man-made version of a burr.

would be covered in loops of thread. When put together, the hooked piece would attach to the looped piece.

He first created a fastener out of cotton. But cotton is very soft. It could only be used a few times. De Mestral wanted to make his invention stronger. He discovered **nylon** fabric worked best. Nylon could be made into strong hooks that could be used again and again.

Make a Guess!

What do you think the word *Velcro* means? Write down your guess. Read on and find out where the word actually comes from. Were you close?

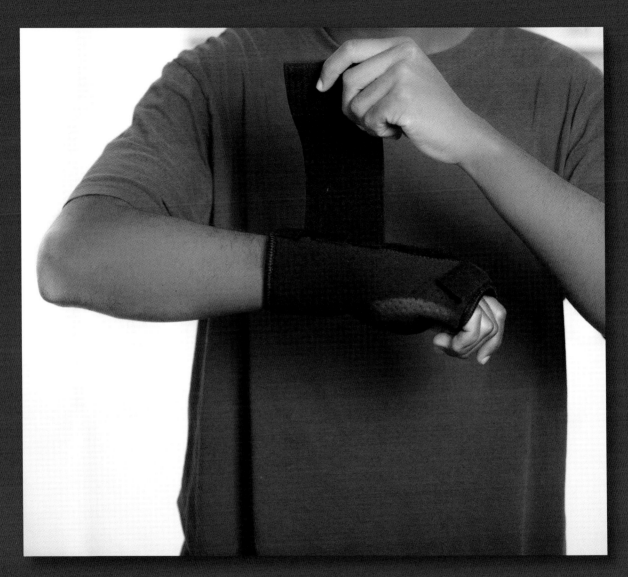

Did you know Velcro is also used to help injured people?

All Kinds of Uses

In 1955, the fastener was finally complete! De Mestral named it Velcro. *Velcro* is a combination of two French words meaning "velvet" and "hook."

He was inspired by the special features of the burr. His invention was based on the concept of **biomimicry**. Biomimicry is a rapidly growing scientific field of research.

Inventors have found many uses for de Mestral's amazing fastener.

Velcro is in space!

One of Velcro's most famous uses is in space. **NASA** uses it on astronauts' space suits and in spaceships. There is no **gravity** in space! The hook and loop fasteners help hold objects down.

Astronauts use Velcro to attach tools to their clothes. This keeps the tools from floating away. Velcro on the bottoms of their shoes helps astronauts keep their feet on the floor.

Think!

What do you use Velcro for? Think about how it helps you. What else do you think you could use Velcro for? Be creative!

Velcro is used in many clothing items.

This incredible invention is everywhere! What amazing new uses will be found for Velcro in the future?

Ask Questions!

Do you have an idea for an invention? Find out what people need. Ask your friends what would make their lives easier. Then, look to nature for inspiration!

GLOSSARY

annoying (uh-NOI-ing) causing trouble

biomimicry (bye-oh-MIM-ik-ree) copying plants and animals to build or improve something

buckle (BUHK-uhl) a metal or plastic device that is attached to one end of a belt or strap and connects it to the other end

connection (kuh-NEK-shuhn) a place where two parts meet and attach to each other

fasteners (FAS-uh-nurz) things that attach other things together

gravity (GRAV-ih-tee) the force that pulls things toward the center of the earth and keeps them from floating away

inspired (in-SPYRD) gave someone an idea for a creation based on something else

NASA (NAS-uh) the National Aeronautics and Space Administration, a U.S. government organization that is responsible for space travel and research

nylon (NYE-lahn) a strong man-made fabric used to make things

FIND OUT MORE

BOOKS

Boccador, Sabine. *Science and Inventions*. Hauppauge, NY: Barron's Educational Series, 2018.

Lanier, Wendy Hinote. *Clothing Inspired by Nature*. Mendota Heights, MN: Focus Readers, 2018.

WEBSITES

PBS Loop Scoops—How We Know So Much About Velcro
http://pbskids.org/loopscoops/about-velcro.html
Find out more about Velcro and how it changed the world.

Science News for Students—Inspired by Nature
www.sciencenewsforstudents.org/article/inspired-nature
Learn more about how nature has helped us discover new technology.

INDEX

A

astronauts, 19

B

biomimicry, 17
buckles, 7
burrs, 9, 10, 11
    and Velcro,
        13–15, 17
buttons, 7

C

clothing, 20

D

de Mestral, George,
    13–15, 17

F

fasteners, 6–9

N

NASA, 18–19
nylon fabric, 15

P

plants, 11, 13

S

seeds, 11, 13
shoelaces, 7
space, 18–19

V

Velcro, 12
    and burrs, 9, 13–15,
        17
    and clothing, 20
    in space, 18–19
    uses for, 4, 5, 16–21
    where the name
        comes from, 17

Z

zippers, 9

ABOUT THE AUTHOR

Jennifer Colby is a school librarian in Ann Arbor, Michigan. She loves reading, traveling, and going to museums to learn about new things.